Irène Lassus and Marie-Anne Voituriez

D1146219

Little Decorations
using Polymer Clay

SEARCH PRESS

Contents

Materials

1 Special decorative paint, available in gloss and matt and a variety of colours

2 Paintbrushes of various sizes

3 Fine sandpaper

4 A large paintbrush for dusting

5 Transparent gel glue

6 Liquid varnish (also available as a spray)

7 Oven thermometer

8 Retractable craft knife

9 Scalpel

10 Metal ruler

11 Lengths of cardboard to use as guides

12 Sheet of glass to use as a work surface for modelling the clay and baking it

13 Wooden skewers

14 Spatulas or chisels

15 Wooden rolling pin for rolling out the modelling clay

16 Oven-bake modelling clay

17 Softening clay

18 Very light, white air-dry clay

19 Air-dry clay that turns white as it dries

Basic techniques

Knead the oven-bake modelling clay and the various air-dry clays on a sheet of glass. The sheet of glass can be used as both a work surface and a baking tray. Make sure you clean it regularly using a glass-cleaning product so the modelling clay doesn't stick. Clean it well, particularly before each colour change.

Make sure you use glass that is sufficiently thick not to break when you apply pressure with the rolling pin or when it is in the oven.

Air-dry clay

There are several different types of air-dry clay; it doesn't matter which you use. They are not all of the same consistency and choosing between them is really a question of personal preference. This sort of clay is generally used for larger items. It is particularly well suited to modelling but can also be rolled out and shaped with a craft knife. Allow 12 to 24 hours for drying. Drying time will depend on the thickness of the model. As air-dry clay is white, it can be painted the desired colour after it has dried.

To avoid the need for too much sanding, it is a good idea to smooth down air-dry clay with water before it dries.

Oven-bake modelling clay

Oven-bake modelling clay does not dry in the air. Until it is baked, it remains pliable and can be re-used. Always keep any leftover clay. Store it in an air-tight box or wrap it in silver foil or cellophane.

Always start by kneading the clay to soften it up. This will make it easier to model by hand or roll out with a rolling pin. The pliability of the clay makes it possible to produce openwork decorations.

You can create multicoloured models by laying sheets of different coloured modelling clay on top of each other, without them merging: this is the millefiori technique (see page 15). You can also superimpose colours (see the Multicoloured candle holder on page 18).

Different colours can also be blended together to get new shades (see page 15).

Baking

Bake the modelling clay on a sheet of glass. Preheat the oven to 130°C (250°F, gas mark 1/2), then put the model in the oven for a maximum of 30 minutes, ensuring the temperature remains constant. Never exceed the baking time or temperature: harmful smoke can be given off. You could use an oven thermometer to be on the safe side.

> **Warning!** Never use a microwave oven to bake the modelling clay.

The clay shrinks slightly on baking. Once baked, models can be washed. They are waterproof.

Softening

Some qualities of modelling clay require the use of softening clay. This is always white.

Blend it with the coloured modelling clay until you get a consistent colour. When used in small quantities, the softening clay does not change the clay's colour.

Modelling

The ball

Take a piece of modelling clay. After conditioning the clay by kneading, roll it into a ball between your hands. Then roll the ball on the glass sheet with the palm of your hand, without pressing down, to ensure it is even. Continue in this way until you get the size ball that you require.

The sausage

Start by making a clay ball then roll it between your hands to elongate it. Then roll it with both hands on the glass sheet until you get the diameter and length you want. Make sure the diameter of the sausage is regular.

The sheet

Make a ball of modelling clay, then roll it out with a rolling pin. Stop when your sheet is of the desired thickness. To ensure the sheet is the same thickness all over, put the cardboard guides on either side of the clay you are rolling out. When the rolling pin comes to rest on these guides, the thickness of the modelling clay block will be the same as the thickness of the guides.

Shaping

Cutting out

Oven-bake modelling clay can easily be cut out with a craft knife or scalpel that makes clean, precise cuts. A scalpel is the best tool for cutting out a pattern, whether freehand or using a template. The craft knife is more useful for cutting strips using a ruler. Always check that the craft knife blade is sharp.

Modelling by hand

Start with a ball of clay or a sausage, then pinch or press as required to achieve the desired shape.

Finishing touches

You can decorate your modelling-clay creations with patterns, veins or holes.

You can use different sized skewers, needles or pins for this before the model is baked or dried (depending on the type of modelling clay used). Air-dry clay can be smoothed down with water while it is still wet.

After baking

Wait five minutes after you have taken the objects out of the oven. The modelling clay should still be soft and you won't risk burning yourself. Peel off the greaseproof paper.

Sanding down

Different modelling clays can be smoothed off using fine sandpaper, after drying or baking. Dust off with a big paintbrush before painting.

Painting

Use acrylic paint in the colour of your choice. Paint using a soft brush, after the object has been dried or baked (depending on the kind of modelling clay you have used). If you use special decorative paint, a single coat should be enough.

Adding a paint effect

Once you have finished your objects (whether baked or dried), you can use a paint effect to give the final touches. Put a little pure acrylic paint on your paintbrush and apply it to the object. Then work with a cloth to give the desired effect.

Varnishing

After baking or drying (depending on the type of modelling clay), you can varnish what you have made. This will provide a glossy finish and a protective coating. Apply two coats of varnish with a soft paintbrush. Leave to dry thoroughly between each coat.

Colours

Modelling clay comes in a wide variety of bright and cheerful colours. You can mix colours together to create new shades. Always start with a test run on a small quantity of modelling clay to check that the result won't be dirty looking or drab. This avoids spoiling too much clay.

Contrasts

By juxtaposing very different colours you create contrast. For example, if you put layers of contrasting colours on top of each other (in this case green, red and yellow), you can then cut them into slices. You can also make spirals in contrasting colours (here pink and blue).

Colour palettes

Contrasts may not always be the effect you are after. You might prefer harmonising shades of the same colour palette, to fit with a general colour scheme. For example, you could add decorations within the same colour range by applying small red and mauve balls to a pink background. You can also make decorations using related tones by putting together sheets of modelling clay in varying shades of a particular colour.

Blending

If you don't have a particular colour, or you want to make a particular shade, you can blend two colours of modelling clay together.

Knead your two colours together until you get a new uniform colour. Adding white will give you pastel shades. Adding black will give you darker shades.

Table of colours
Combinations of primary colours:

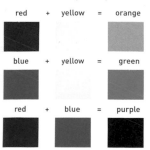

red	+	yellow	=	orange
blue	+	yellow	=	green
red	+	blue	=	purple

Millefiori

The colours and plasticity of oven-bake modelling clay make it the perfect material for creating millefiori, allowing you to set contrasting colours against each other so your pattern stands out.

The basic technique (explained here) will soon have you progressing on to a wide variety of colour variations, forms and patterns. Thin sheets and sausage shapes are the basic starting point for all millefiori decorations.

The spiral

Roll out two thin sheets of clay, lay one on top of the other and then roll them up together to form a spiral pattern.

Striped block

Lay several sheets of clay on top of each other (here red and white). Cut the block obtained into slices and line them up next to each other to get a block of even stripes. If you flatten out a striped block with a rolling pin, you will change the pattern and the thickness of the sheet and the stripes will become wider.

The sun

Wrap a single-colour sausage in a sheet of striped clay. Cut into slices. You will get a sun pattern on each slice.

Patterns

Roll up several sausages made of contrasting colours in a large sheet. Cut the resulting sausage into thin slices.

Arrange the slices next to each other to create a floral pattern.

Flattening out

After putting them together, flatten out the slices with a rolling pin to make a sheet from which you can cut out a pattern.

Multicoloured candle holder

Materials: oven-bake modelling clay in 10 different colours, tealight

Preparing the sheets

On a sheet of glass, roll out around twenty oven-bake clay sheets, to a thickness of around 3mm (⅛in) and measuring 10cm (4in) down each side. Lay them one on top of the other, alternating the colours harmoniously.

Cutting the candle-holder into shape

Cut out a square of paper, measuring 8cm (3¼in) along each side. Place it on the pile of sheets of modelling clay. Centre it carefully. Using the ruler and the craft knife (with the blade extended as far as possible), cut along each side of the square in a single clean slice.

Putting the candle into place

Pinpoint the centre of the square by drawing in the diagonals very lightly with a skewer. Mark the position of the candle using the metal part of the tealight. With the help of a scalpel, cut round this circle, section by section. Continue to hollow out the centre until you get a hole the height of the tealight. Slip the metal casing from the tealight inside the candle-holder and put in the oven to bake.

Butterfly photo holder

Materials: very light white air-dry clay, special decorative paint in green, pink, salmon and orange, thin wire, 3 small flower pots

Cutting out the butterflies

Trace the butterfly pattern (page 23) and transfer it to thin cardboard. Cut it out. On a glass sheet, roll out a block of air-dry clay with a rolling pin, to a thickness of around 3mm (⅛in). Put the template on the clay and cut round the shape carefully with a scalpel three times. Cut out the patterns on the butterflies' wings, but leave the third one plain.

Making the antennae

For each butterfly, cut two lengths of wire, one 25cm (9¾in) long and the other 15cm (6in). Make spirals at one end of each piece of wire, using pliers. Push the two pieces of wire into the middle section of each butterfly to form the antennae. The longer piece of wire, by being pushed right through and out of the other side, will be used to fix the butterfly in the pot. Let the butterflies dry before sanding them carefully to get a nice smooth surface.

Preparing the pots
Fill the three little pots with air-dry clay.
Use a piece of wire to make a hole in the centre
so you can insert the butterflies later. Leave to
dry, then paint the pots and the clay inside
them green.

Assembly
Paint the three butterflies
pink, salmon and orange
respectively. Leave to dry.
Insert the butterflies into
the pots by pushing the wire
supports into the holes. You
can add a drop of glue to
make sure they stay in place.
Likewise if the antennae are a
bit loose, add a drop of glue.

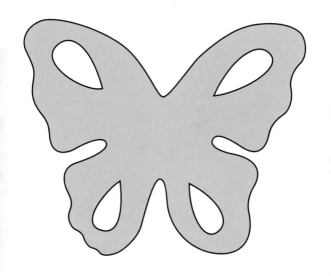

Pop-art flower vase

Materials: yellow, dark pink and orange oven-bake modelling clay

Cutting out the petals

Trace the suggested petal patterns (page 26–27) and transfer them onto thin cardboard. Cut out. On a glass sheet, roll out a block of orange oven-bake modelling clay with a rolling pin, making it as thin as possible. Put the template for the large petals onto the clay and cut round the shape carefully using a scalpel. Make approximately ten large petals in each colour in this way. Do the same using the template for the small petals.

Assembling the flower
Shape the base of all the petals into a point so they can be arranged next to each other to form the flower. Using a pin, trace veins onto the petals, for the orange flower only. Assemble the flower by laying the big petals next to each other to form a crown. Place the smaller petals on top. Use a spatula to help. Lift the top petals slightly to give the flower some volume. For the middle of the flower, make a small flattened ball and prick a

pattern onto it using a pin. Press it into place. You could also stick tiny balls of modelling clay onto the centre of the flower.

Orange flower

Yellow flower

Sticking together

Bake the flower. After it has cooled, use transparent gel glue to stick it onto a vase, around 2cm (¾in) from the top edge.

Dark pink flower

Hanging angels

Materials: white oven-bake modelling clay, 4 feathers, silver wire, transparent ribbon, white thread

Cutting out the angel
Trace the angel pattern (page 31) and transfer it onto thin cardboard. Cut out. On a glass sheet, roll out a block of white oven-bake modelling clay with a rolling pin, to a thickness of 2mm (1/16 in). Put the template onto the clay and carefully cut round the shape using a scalpel.

Making the halo and decorating
Use a small coin to cut out the halo.
Put the coin onto the clay and carefully
cut around it using a scalpel. Cut out
the centre of the halo. Using the
rounded end of a skewer make the
small holes shown on the template.
Round out and smooth the hole using
the pointed end of the skewer. Make a
little hole towards the top of the head
so you can attach the halo. Bake. Sand
down carefully.

Assembly
Glue four feathers onto
the back of the angel for
wings. Wrap silver wire
round the halo and fix it
through the hole in the
head. Place it horizontally.
Tie a transparent ribbon
round the neck of the
angel. Make as many
angels as desired and
hang them up using
white thread.

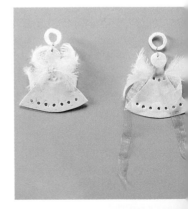

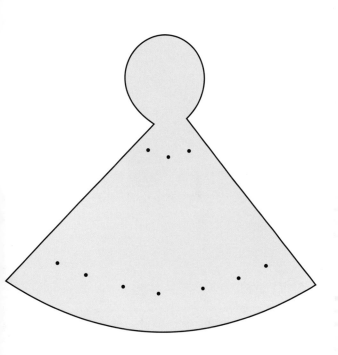

Candy drawer knobs

Materials: miniature chest of 6 drawers and drawer handle screws

Materials for the English rock candy: turquoise, pink, yellow, orange and black oven-bake modelling clay

Materials for the square boiled sweet: black, fluorescent green, yellow and pink oven-bake modelling clay

Materials for the liquorice roll: turquoise and black oven-bake modelling clay

Materials for the red and yellow sweet: red and yellow oven-bake modelling clay

Materials for the candy bar: pink and yellow oven-bake modelling clay

For the candy cane: red and white oven-bake modelling clay

English rock candy
Making the sweet

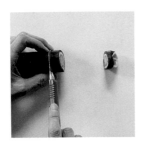

On a glass sheet, roll out blocks of turquoise, pink, yellow and black clay to a thickness of 2mm (1/16 in). Roll an orange sausage around 5mm (1/4in) in diameter. Wrap a sheet of turquoise clay round this sausage. Cut it so the edges abut. Wrap this new sausage in a layer of pink clay in the same way, then a yellow layer and finish with a black layer. Smooth the ends together where they meet. Using a craft knife, cut off the end of the sausage, then cut into slices around 5mm (1/4in) thick.

Attaching the screw

Using a skewer, make a hole in the centre of one side of the sweet. Push the drawer handle screw into the hole. Cover the screw-head by smoothing the clay around it with a spatula. Bake.

Square boiled sweet

Preparing the layers

On a glass sheet, use a rolling pin to roll out blocks of black, fluorescent green, yellow and pink clay to a thickness of 2mm (1/16 in). Lay them on top of each other, alternating colours. Start and finish with a layer of black.

Cutting

Using a ruler and craft knife, carefully cut out a rectangle to the required size. Put the screw into place (see 'Attaching the screw' above). Bake.

Liquorice roll

Softening

Start by mixing a ball of black clay with some softening clay (see 'Basic techniques' on page 9). Your clay should then be more pliable and easier to model.

Making the ribbon

Make a black clay sausage. Put two 2mm (1/16 in)-high cardboard guides on either side of the sausage and flatten it with a rolling pin to obtain a strip 2mm (1/16 in) thick. With the help of a ruler, cut the strip to a width of 5mm (¼in). Cut one of the ends off cleanly.

Shaping

Make a little ball with turquoise clay. Roll the black strip around the ball until it is of the required diameter. Cut the end of the strip off cleanly and detach it slightly from the rest of the roll. Put the screw into place (see 'Attaching the screw', page 34). Bake.

Red and yellow sweet
Making the sweet

Roll a red ball in the palm of your hand. Roll some tiny balls of yellow modelling clay. Dot them all over the red ball and roll it in the palm of your hand so they are embedded. Flatten the sweet slightly.

Making the wrapper

With a rolling pin, flatten out two blocks of red clay and two blocks of yellow clay, to a thickness of 2mm (1/16 in). Lay them on top of each other, alternating colours. Cut two slices and then cut those into a triangle.

Putting the wrapper into place

Using a skewer, make a hole in each side of the sweet and insert the pointed end of the wrappers. Put the screw into place (see 'Attaching the screw', page 34). Bake.

Candy bar

Modelling

Shape one rectangle from pink clay and two from yellow clay. Start off by rolling a sausage in the desired colour. Then with a craft knife, cut it into a three-dimensional rectangle.

Assembling the sweet

Put the pink segment between the two yellow ones and press them together. Smooth the joins with your finger. Push into shape by pressing each side down onto the glass sheet.

The wrappers

Make the wrappers as per the instructions for the red and yellow sweet, by laying pink and yellow sheets of clay on top of each other. Stick them to the ends of the candy bar. Put the screw into place (see 'Attaching the screw', page 34). Bake.

Candy cane

Modelling

Make one white clay sausage, 1cm (½in) in diameter, and one very thin red sausage. Wind the red sausage around the white one. Roll them together so that the red decoration becomes embedded in the white clay.

Finishing touches

Cut off the two ends with a craft knife. Bend over one end to make a walking-stick shape. Put the screw into place (see 'Attaching the screw', page 34). Bake.

Millefiori buttons

Materials: red, yellow, blue, pink and dark green oven-bake modelling clay

The central spiral

On a glass sheet, roll out a block of red modelling clay with a rolling pin, to a thickness of around 2mm (1/16 in). Roll out a second identical block of yellow modelling clay. Lay the two sheets on top of each other and roll them up together to get the central spiral.

The petals

Make an even, yellow sausage, 1cm (1/2in) in diameter and 10cm (4in) in length. Roll out a sheet of blue modelling clay, 2mm (1/16 in) thick. Wrap the yellow sausage in this sheet. Roll out this new sausage until it is around 20cm (7¾in) long. Make sure that it remains even.

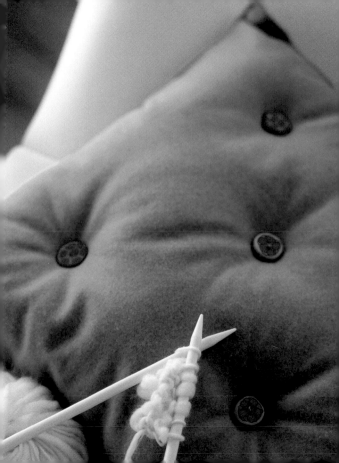

The triangles

Make the triangles that separate the petals.
Make a pink sausage, 1cm (½in) in diameter
and 20cm (7¾in) long. Pinch it slightly to
give it a triangular shape. With a craft knife,
cut the yellow and blue sausage for the
petals into five pieces, each around 4cm
(1½in) long. Likewise cut the pink triangular
sausage into five.

Putting the flower together

Put the yellow and blue petals around
the central (red and yellow) spiral. Put a
pink triangle between each petal of blue
and yellow.

The outside

Roll out a sheet of dark green modelling
clay, 2mm (1/16 in) thick. Wrap the flower in
this sheet. Roll the resulting sausage until
its diameter is around 2cm (¾in) and it
measures 10cm (4in) to 12cm (4¾in)
in length.

Cutting

Using a craft knife, cut the sausage into
3mm (1/8in) thick slices. Use a skewer to
make two button holes in the centre of each
slice. Bake.

Variation: Millefiori eggs

Assembling the pattern
Follow the same procedure as for the buttons (page 38–40). Stop when you get to the cutting stage. Cut ten 3mm (⅛in) thick slices from the sausage shape. Arrange them next to each other on the glass sheet.

Shaping
Using a rolling pin, flatten the whole thing. Turn it all over, then flatten the other side.

Cutting out the shape
Enlarge the egg pattern provided to 200 per cent and transfer it onto thin cardboard. Cut it out. Put the template on the millefiori and cut out the shape carefully using a scalpel. Before baking, make a hole 1cm (½in) from the edge of the top of the egg with a skewer so that you can add a bow tied with a narrow ribbon later. Bake.

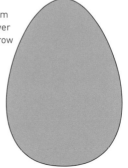

Contrasting colours

Make other eggs in the same way, but changing the starting colours: for the egg at the top right, use green, pink, fuchsia, blue and light green oven-bake modelling clay; for the one at the bottom right, use turquoise, pink, yellow, blue and green oven-bake modelling clay.

Miniature wardrobe

Materials: white air-dry modelling clay, special decorative paint in light green, turquoise, pink, yellow, blue and pearly mauve, thin wire, foam board

Making the clothes hangers
Using wire cutters, cut a 10cm (4in) length of wire. Make a small clothes hanger, measuring 3cm (1¼in) along the base, by twisting the wire. Use pliers to help you. Make four little clothes hangers in this way.

Cutting out the clothes
On a glass sheet, roll out a plaque of air-dry clay with a rolling pin, to a thickness of around 4mm (⅛in). Enlarge the patterns for the clothes (page 48) to 200 per cent and transfer them to thin cardboard. Cut out. Put the templates onto the clay and cut out the shapes using a scalpel.

Assembly
Push the clothes hanger down into the top of the item of clothing and make sure it is lying flat. Smooth over with a little bit of water. Leave to dry.

The boots

Roll out a small sausage, 5cm (2in) in length, 1cm (½in) in diameter. Bend the sausage at a right angle 2cm (¾in) from one end. Insert the skewer into the remaining 3cm (1¼in) and mould the boot around the skewer. Smooth over with a little bit of water. Enlarge the central hole and leave to dry.

The hats

Make a small ball and a sausage. Use water to stick the sausage round the ball. Model into shape and push your thumb into the middle to make the head hole. Smooth over with a little bit of water. Leave to dry.

The boxes and the basket

Make the cuboid box shapes from small balls that you then square off by pressing lightly against the glass sheet. For the basket, make a small ball, then hollow out the inside. Smooth over with a little bit of water. Leave to dry.

The clothes bag

Roll out a block of modelling clay, to a thickness of 5mm (¼in). Cut out three pieces measuring 3 × 3cm (1¼ x1¼in), and three others measuring 3 × 4.5cm (1¼in x1¾in) for the various items of clothing.

Enlarge the pattern for the bag (page 48) to 200 per cent and transfer it to thin cardboard. Cut out. Put the template on the clay and carefully cut round the shape using a scalpel. Smooth over with a little bit of water. Leave to dry.

The wardrobe

The mouldings and the feet of the wardrobe

For the decorative mouldings, make small sausages that you can curl into arabesques and some small balls flattened on one side. Make four slightly larger balls for the wardrobe's feet. Leave to dry.

Sanding down and painting

When everything is completely dry, sand down carefully and then paint. Flick through a magazine if you need some inspiration for colours. Make

sure the paint is completely dry before you attach anything.

Making the wardrobe

Trace the patterns on pages 48 – 49, and use a craft knife to cut out the different parts of the wardrobe from 5mm (¼in) thick foam board. Join them together with glue. Paint the wardrobe light blue. Cut a wooden skewer to the right length to make the rail. Paint it blue and glue it in place. Glue on the feet and the mouldings and arrange the different items in the wardrobe as desired.

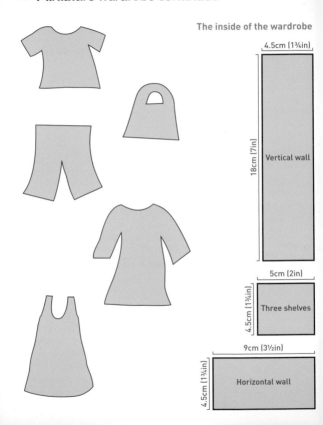

The inside of the wardrobe

4.5cm (1¾in)

18cm (7in)

Vertical wall

5cm (2in)

4.5cm (1¾in)

Three shelves

9cm (3½in)

4.5cm (1¾in)

Horizontal wall

The outside of the wardrobe

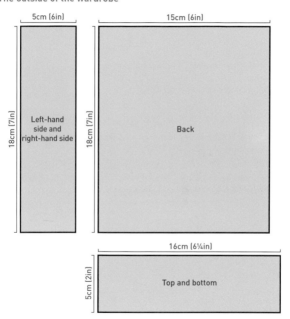

5cm (6in)

Left-hand side and right-hand side

18cm (7in)

15cm (6in)

18cm (7in)

Back

16cm (6¼in)

5cm (2in)

Top and bottom

Charm necklace

Materials: red, pink and turquoise oven-bake modelling clay, thin wire, jewellery cord, silver beads, necklace clasp, silver charms

Modelling the charms

Roll some small balls of modelling clay. Make circles, hearts and stars from these balls, approximately 3mm (⅛in) thick. Decorate the centre of the star and circle with a tiny ball of a different colour clay. Push it gently into the centre of the charm.

Making the attachments

Cut some 2cm (¾in) lengths of wire to make the attachments. Bend the wire in half and push the two ends into the top of the charm.

Baking and varnishing

Bake all the charms. Allow them to cool before varnishing. Leave to dry.

Threading

Cut two 50cm (19¾in) lengths of jewellery cord. Thread two silver beads onto the two cords together, then a clay charm onto a single cord. Continue in this way, alternating clay charms with silver ones, until you have the desired length. Finish off with a row of silver beads at each end. Cut off any leftover cord and attach a clasp.

Gilded jewellery

Materials: jewellery mounts for earrings, jump rings, brooches, hair slide; very light, white air-dry clay, gilding paint

Cutting out the patterns
Trace the different leaf patterns (page 54–55) and transfer them to thin cardboard. Cut out. On a glass sheet, roll out a block of air-dry clay with a rolling pin, to a thickness of around 2mm (1/16 in). Put the leaf templates onto the clay and cut round the shapes carefully with a scalpel. Cut a rectangular strip of clay the right length and width for the hair slide. Stick it onto the hair slide mount.

Drawing the veins
Using a skewer, trace the veins onto the leaves using the templates as guides. Using the skewer again, make holes in the top edge of the earring leaves. Use these for the attachments.

Assembly
Put the leaves aside to dry. Then paint everything using the gilding paint. When the paint is dry, glue the leaves onto the brooch and hair slide mounts. Attach the earring hooks using jump rings.

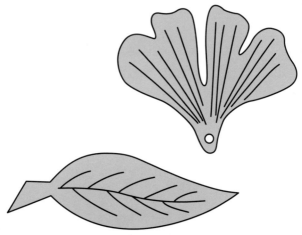

Millefiori necklaces

Materials: mauve, blue, pink, orange, red and white oven-bake modelling clay; yellow and red cords

The mauve bead necklace

Preparing the modelling clay

On a glass sheet, roll out blocks of blue, pink and orange modelling clay with a rolling pin, to a thickness of around 2mm (1/16 in). Make a sausage with the mauve clay, 1cm (1/2in) in diameter. Wrap this sausage in the sheet of blue modelling clay. Smooth over the ends where they meet.

Putting the sheets of clay together
Now wrap the blue sausage you have just made in the sheet of orange modelling clay. Finish with the sheet of pink modelling clay. Roll this sausage to elongate it, then using a craft knife, cut it into six pieces.

Making the pattern
Take one of the pieces and place the other five pieces round it to make a flower. Roll this flower into a smooth, longer sausage and put aside.

Making the beads
Now roll a pink and mauve sausage and cut both into pieces. Make as many beads as you need in this way. Cut the sausage obtained in the previous stage into very thin circles. Wrap three of these circles on each bead. Thread the beads onto a skewer and roll them on the glass sheet so the pattern is fully embedded. Bake them on the skewer.

Threading
When the beads are baked, allow them to cool. Slide them off the skewer and thread them onto a yellow cotton cord. Finish with a knot.

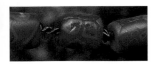

The pink and red bead necklace

In the same way as before, start with a sausage (this time in red) and wrap it in a sheet of blue, rather than pink, and finish with a sheet of red. As before, stick the thin round patterns onto red and pink clay beads. Skewer them and bake. Thread the beads onto a red cotton cord, making a knot between each bead.

The round-bead necklace

The round beads are made in a similar way to the previous ones. For the decoration, start with a blue sausage, wrap it in an orange sheet and then a pink one. Stick the thin round patterns onto round red and pink clay beads. Skewer them and bake. Thread the beads onto a yellow cotton cord, making a knot between each bead.

Variation: the red and white bead necklace

Laying sheets on top of each other
On a glass sheet, roll out a block of red
modelling clay with a rolling pin, to a
thickness of around 2mm (1/16 in), and
another of white modelling clay. Lay
one of the sheets on top of the other.
Cut in half with a craft knife and lay
one half on top of the other,
alternating the colours. Ensure the
block of clay is of an even height.

Making the striped block
Using a craft knife and a ruler, cut
striped slices around 2mm (1/16 in)
thick cleanly from the block. Put the
slices together to get a red and white
striped block. Flatten gently with a
rolling pin to even out.

Putting the block into place
Roll a red clay sausage
around 1cm (1/2in) in diameter.
Wrap it in the stripy sheet of
modelling clay. Roll the
sausage obtained to
elongate it.

Making the beads

Roll a red clay sausage 1cm (½in) in diameter. Cut into pieces, each of which will form a bead. Also slice some thin round slices to put between each red and white bead.

Cut thin slices from the stripy sausage and use them to decorate the red beads by sticking three patterns onto each red bead.

Finishing touches

Thread the beads onto a skewer and roll them on the glass sheet to flatten them out and so the pattern is fully embedded in the bead. Bake all the beads while they are still on the skewer.

Threading

When the beads are baked, allow them to cool. Remove them from the skewer and thread them onto a red cotton cord. Alternate the thin red flat circles and the red and white beads. Make a knot between each item. Finish with a knot.

First published in Great Britian in 2015 by
Search Press Ltd.
Wellwood, North Farm Road,
Tunbridge Wells,
Kent, TN2 3DR

Copyright © Larousse 2012
© Dessain et Tolra / SEJER 2004
Original French title published as *Petites Décos en pâte polymère*

English translation by Burravoe Translation Services

Typesetting by Greengate Publishing Services, Tonbridge, Kent

ISBN: 978-1-78221-245-4

Photographs: Francis Waldman
Styling: Pascale Chombart de Lauwe
Photography credit: Photogravure Turquoise, Émerainville

Printed in China